by Louise Nelson

Minneapolis, Minnesota

**Credits**: All images are courtesy of Shutterstock.com, unless otherwise specified. With thanks to Getty Images, Thinkstock Photo, and iStockphoto. Cover – Warpaint, Konstantin G, Julia-art, Nikulina Tatiana, Zdenek Klucka. Images used on every page – Julia-art, Wetzkaz Graphics, Nikulina Tatiana, Zdenek Klucka. 2 – Warpaint. 4–5 – Catmando, Dotted Yeti, Orla. 6–7 – Herschel Hoffmeyer, Viktorya170377. 8–9 – Herschel Hoffmeyer, Martin Weber, © Kevmin/Wikimedia Creative Commons license 3.0. 10–11 – Michael Rosskothen, Warpaint. 12–13 – Daniel Eskridge, Michael Rosskothen. 14–15 – Catmando. 16–17 – Daniel Eskridge, Dotted Yeti, Martin Pelanek. 18–19 – Daniel Eskridge, James Wagstaff. 20–21 – Mark_ Kostich, paleontologist natural. 22–23 – Ekaterina Verbis, Warpaint.

Library of Congress Cataloging-in-Publication Data is available at www.loc.gov or upon request from the publisher.

ISBN: 979-8-88509-365-1 (hardcover)
ISBN: 979-8-88509-487-0 (paperback)
ISBN: 979-8-88509-602-7 (ebook)

© 2023 Booklife Publishing
This edition is published by arrangement with Booklife Publishing.

North American adaptations © 2023 Bearport Publishing Company. All rights reserved. No part of this publication may be reproduced in whole or in part, stored in any retrieval system, or transmitted in any form or by any means, electronic, mechanical, photocopying, recording, or otherwise, without written permission from the publisher.

For more information, write to Bearport Publishing, 5357 Penn Avenue South, Minneapolis, MN 55419.

# CONTENTS

A Time of Powerful Beasts . . . . . . . . . 4

The Pleistocene Epoch . . . . . . . . . . . . 6

Dinosaurs of the Pleistocene . . . . . . . 8

Not a Dino. . . . . . . . . . . . . . . . . . . . . 10

How Do We Know? . . . . . . . . . . . . . . 12

*Megaloceros* . . . . . . . . . . . . . . . . . . 14

Woolly Mammoth . . . . . . . . . . . . . . . 16

Giant Ground Sloth. . . . . . . . . . . . . . 18

*Glyptodon* . . . . . . . . . . . . . . . . . . . . . 20

End of the Pleistocene . . . . . . . . . . . 22

Glossary . . . . . . . . . . . . . . . . . . . . . . 24

Index . . . . . . . . . . . . . . . . . . . . . . . . . 24

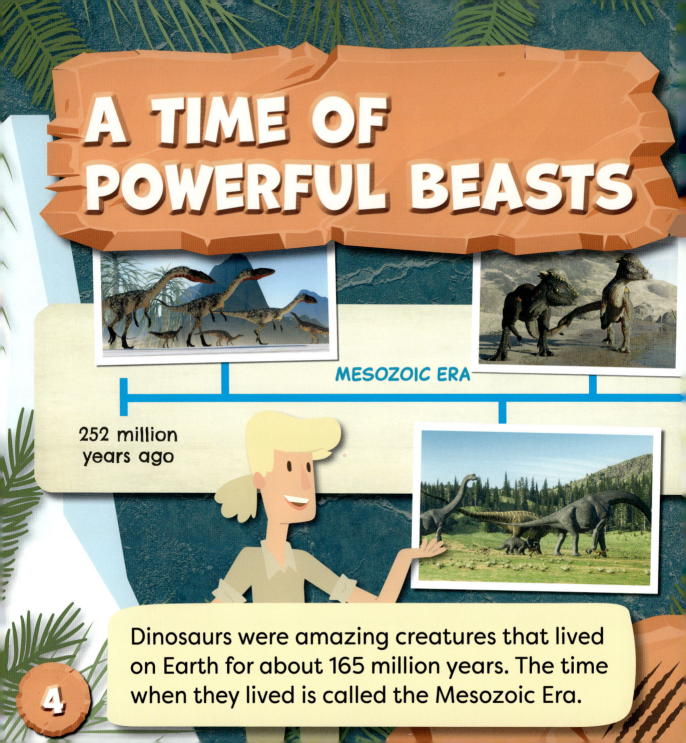

# A TIME OF POWERFUL BEASTS

MESOZOIC ERA

252 million years ago

Dinosaurs were amazing creatures that lived on Earth for about 165 million years. The time when they lived is called the Mesozoic Era.

After dinosaurs, other large animals appeared. The Cenozoic Era is the time from the end of the dinosaurs to the present day. Near the end of this era is the Pleistocene epoch.

CENOZOIC ERA

66 million years ago

Pleistocene epoch

Present day

The Pleistocene epoch lasted from 2 million to 11 thousand years ago.

5

During this frozen time, many creatures had thick fur to stay warm. Early humans began to **evolve**, too.

# DINOSAURS OF THE PLEISTOCENE

Most dinosaurs became **extinct** by the end of the Mesozoic era. The only group that survived were birds. All birds alive today came from those dinosaurs.

A skeleton of *Dromornis*

Giant birds known as thunder birds roamed the land during the Pleistocene. They ate mostly plants and were so big they could not fly. These birds lived at the same time as early humans.

# NOT A DINO

Many large animals lived during the Pleistocene epoch. But they weren't dinos! Dinosaurs are a specific group of animals. All dinosaurs are **reptiles**.

10

# HOW DO WE KNOW?

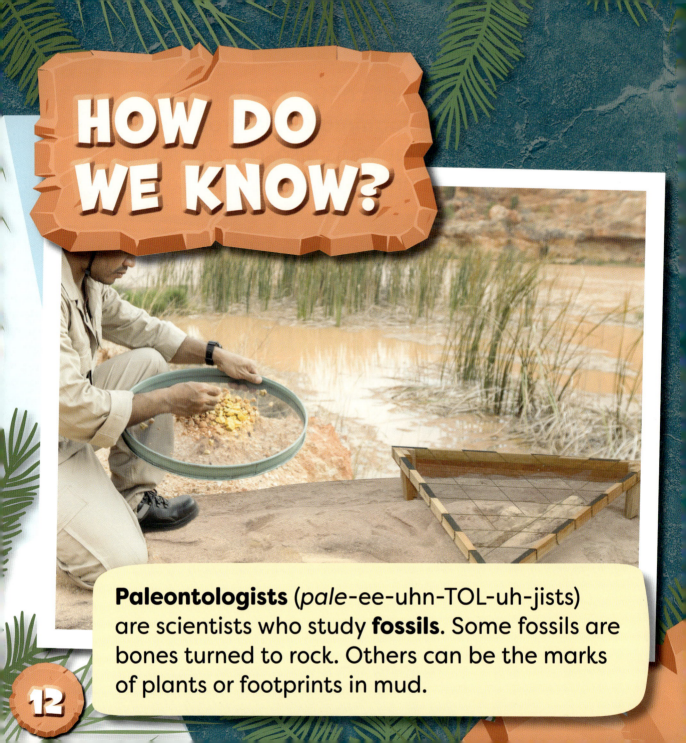

**Paleontologists** (*pale*-ee-uhn-TOL-uh-jists) are scientists who study **fossils**. Some fossils are bones turned to rock. Others can be the marks of plants or footprints in mud.

## A Quick Look

### Giant Deer
*Megaloceros* was one of the largest deer that ever lived.

### Plant Eater
These animals did not eat meat.

### Huge Antlers
*Megaloceros* had antlers almost as wide as the length of a car!

*Megaloceros* was a giant animal, but it was NOT a dinosaur.

## A Quick Look

### Picture Perfect
Old cave paintings show groups of woolly mammoths.

### Plant Eaters
These animals ate plants that grew in their frozen home.

### Alive Again?
Scientists want to bring a woolly mammoth back to life using old **DNA** they found.

The woolly mammoth was a kind of elephant. It was NOT a dinosaur.

## A Quick Look

### Huge Size
Some giant ground sloths could grow as big as elephants!

### Mostly a Plant Eater
These animals ate vegetables, grasses, and leaves. But some may have also eaten meat.

### Sloths in Trees
The sloths alive today are much smaller and live in trees.

Three-toed sloth

This giant was NOT a dinosaur.

## A Quick Look

**Car Size**
Glyptodon was as big as a small car.

**Plant and Bug Eater**
These animals ate plants and sometimes insects.

**Hard Shell**
Glyptodon had a hard shell and tail.

*Glyptodon* looked like some dinosaurs. But it was NOT a dino.

# END OF THE PLEISTOCENE

Many animals became extinct at the end of the Pleistocene epoch. Humans may have caused part of this by hunting so many large animals.

Humans were spreading all over Earth by the end of the Pleistocene. This was the time when people began to rule.

# GLOSSARY

**DNA** tiny things that tell how to make up a living thing

**evolve** to change or develop slowly

**extinct** no longer existing

**fossils** bones, teeth, or other things from life long ago

**mammals** warm-blooded animals with hair or fur, whose babies drink milk from the mother's body

**paleontologists** scientists who study fossils to find out about life in the past

**reptiles** cold-blooded animals that breathe air and have scaly skin

# INDEX

birds 8–9
cave paintings 17
epochs 5–6, 10, 22
eras 4–5, 8
fossils 12–13
humans 7, 9, 11, 22–23
ice 6
mammals 11, 18